English Fragments
from
Latin Medieval Service-Books.

Early English Text Society,

Extra Series, XC.

NOTE.

THE facsimiles of this little pamphlet explain themselves. The Manual, which was the medieval priest's handbook for the services of Baptism, Marriage, Visitation of the Sick, Burial, etc., is virtually the only one of the medieval Latin service-books which contained invariably a certain proportion of its text in English. The text of the English varies in a measure in different MSS.

English Fragments
from
Latin Medieval Service-Books

WITH

FACSIMILES

FROM

Mediebal Prymers.

EDITED BY

HENRY LITTLEHALES.

LONDON:
PUBLISHED FOR THE EARLY ENGLISH TEXT SOCIETY
By KEGAN PAUL, TRENCH, TRÜBNER & CO., LIMITED,
DRYDEN HOUSE, 43, GERRARD STREET, SOHO, W.

OXFORD
UNIVERSITY PRESS

Great Clarendon Street, Oxford OX2 6DP
United Kingdom

Oxford University Press is a department of the University of Oxford.
It furthers the University's objective of excellence in research, scholarship,
and education by publishing worldwide. Oxford is a registered trade mark of
Oxford University Press in the UK and in certain other countries

© The Early English Text Society 1903

The moral rights of the authors have been asserted

Database right Oxford University Press (maker)

First Edition published in 1903
Reprinted 2001

All rights reserved. No part of this publication may be reproduced,
stored in a retrieval system, or transmitted, in any form or by any means,
without the prior permission in writing of Oxford University Press,
or as expressly permitted by law, or under terms agreed with the appropriate
reprographics rights organization. Enquiries concerning reproduction
outside the scope of the above should be sent to the Rights Department,
Oxford University Press, at the address above

You must not circulate this book in any other form
and you must impose this same condition on any acquirer

Published in the United States of America by Oxford University Press
198 Madison Avenue, New York, NY 10016, United States of America

British Library Cataloguing in Publication Data
Data available

Library of Congress Cataloging in Publication Data
Data available

Extra Series, 90

ISBN 978-0-85-991998-2

Mr. Henry Littlehales, who, in 1898, *gave the Chaucer Society his* Notes on the Road from London to Canterbury, *no.* 30 *of the Society's Second Series, and who also edited for the Early English Text Society " The Prymer, or Lay Folk's Prayer-Book," from a Cambridge University MS. ab.* 1420, *nos.* 105, 109 *in the Original Series, has kindly given the Chaucer Society* 250 *copies of each of the Facsimiles of two Illuminated pages in Fifteenth-Century MS. Prymers in the British Museum.*

They are issued herewith, but are not made one of the Society's publications, because we cannot undertake to reproduce them when the present copies run out. Every Member will decide for himself whether he puts these Facsimiles into one of the Society's Texts, or keeps them apart in his picture-album.

All will join in thanking Mr. Littlehales for his pretty and welcome gift.

F. J. Furnivall.

1 August, 1903.

A page of a fifteenth century Prymer, (the common medieval layfolks prayer book) From the Brit. Mus. MS 2 A XVIII.

Full Size.

A page of a fifteenth century Prymer: Brit Mus. MS. Harl. 2915. This is the common picture before the Office for the Dead.

From the British Museum Manual, MS. 30,506 (xv cent.).

FROM THE SERVICE FOR BAPTISM.

[1] N. I cristene þe in þe name of þe fader, and of þe sone, and of þe holy gost.

[2] Godfaderis and godmoderis, I charge ȝow, and þe fader and þe moder, that þis child be kept þis seuen ȝer fro water, fro feer, fro hors [3] fot, fro hondes toth; and þat he ligge not be þe fader an be þe moder vn-to tyme he conne sey "ligge outter," and þat he be confermyd of a byschop that next cometh to contre be seuen myle behalue, and þat [he] be tauȝt his beleue, þat is for to sey, Pater noster, Aue maria, and Credo; And þat ȝe wasche ȝour hondes er ȝe goon owt of chirche, in peyne of fastyng xl fridayes.

FROM THE MARRIAGE SERVICE.

[4] I aske þe banes betwen I de B and A de C. ȝif any man or woman kan sey or put any lettenge of sybrede, wherfor they may not, ne owght not, to come togedere be lawe of holy chirche, do vs to wete.

[5] Lo, syres, we been her gadered togedere befor god and alle his aungelis and his seyntis, in þe sith of holi cherche, to knette togedere two bodies, that is to sey, þis man and þis woman, to þis ende, þat from þis tyme forward þei moste be o flesch, and two sowles in þe feith and in þe lawe of god, to deserue togedere euer lastyng lyf in amendement of that þat þei haue do amys herbefore: wherfor I amones ȝow alle, that, ȝif þer be any of ȝow þat knowe any lawful lettyng whi þis man and þis woman mai not be wedded togedere lawfulli, þat now he sey and knowliche it.

Also I charge ȝow, bothe man and woman, þat ȝif ony of ȝow haue made any contract priuyli [6] before þis tyme, or any avow mad, or ony other cause knowe, whi þat ȝe mai not come to-gedere lawfulli, now knowliche it.

N. Wiltow haue þis woman to þin wyf, and loue here, and worshipe here, and holde hire, and kepe here in seknes and in hele, as an

[1] leaf 23.   [2] leaf 23, back.   [3] leaf 24.   [4] leaf 25.
[5] leaf 25, back.   [6] leaf 26.

6 From the Marriage Service and the Visitation of the Sick.

hosbonde owyth to his wif, and alle oþer women to forsaken for hire, and only to drawe to hire as longe as ȝowre bothe lyues to gedere lasten ?

. . . .

[1] N. Wiltow haue þis man to þin housbonde, to been buxum to hym, and serue hym, and loue hym, and worschipe hym, and kepe hym in syknes and in hele, as a wif owith to do here housbonde, and alle oþer men forsaken for hym, and only to drawe to hym as longe as ȝowre bothyn lyues to-gedere lasten ?

. . . .

I .N. take the N. to myn wedded wyf, to haue and to holde from þis day forward, for beter, for wers, for richere, for porere, for fayrere, for fowlere, in seknes and in helthe, til deth vs departe, ȝif holy chirche it wil ordeyne : and therto I plithe þe myn trewthe.

. . . .

I .N. take the N, to myn weddid housbonde, to haue and to holde from þis day forward, for beter, for wers, for richer, for porere, for fayrere, for fowlere, in seknes and in hele, to be boner and buxum, [2]as a wyf owyd to hur husb[an]dd,[2] til deth vs departe, as holi cherche it [2]wil[2] ordeyne : and therto i plith the myn trowthe.

. . . .

[3] With þis ryng I þe wedde, and þis gold and siluer I þe ȝeue, and with al myn bodi I the worschepe, and with al myn wordlich catel I the honowre.

. .· · . . . .

[1] leaf 26, back. [2—2] In a later hand. [3] leaf 27, back.

FROM THE OFFICE FOR THE VISITATION OF THE SICK.

From the British Museum Manual, MS. 32,320 (XV cent.).

How men þat ben in hele sculde visite sike men.

[4] Beleuyst þow in god, fader almythi, makere of. heuene and of erthe ?

. . . .

I beleue.

Beleuyst þow in his sone, þe secunde persone in trinite, crist

[4] leaf 50, back.

[a] My dere sone or douȝtere in god, hyt semith þat þou hyest þe faste in þe wey fro þis life to godward, þere þou schalt cee al þy forme-fadris, apostelis, martiris, confessouris and uirgynis, & all men and [b]wom-

[a] leaf 13, back. [b] leaf 14.

From the Office for the Visitation of the Sick.

ihesu, the whiche was conseyuyd be þe myght of þe holy gost, and born of þe blessid mayden, owre ladi seynt marie? Credo.

Beleuest thow that he leued here two and thritty ȝer and more, and suffred at þe last, deth on þe cros for þe loue of mankende? Credo.

Beleuyst þow that he wente to helle & took owt adam and eue and the sowles þat were þerynne, the whych myȝth not come to blysse til cristes passioun? Credo.

Beleuyst thow þat he ros vp fro deth on estir day, and dwellede her til ascensioun day, to preue ve¹rily his resurreccioun? Credo.

Beleuyst þow that thanne he styed vp in-to heuene be his myȝth, god and man, and there is euyn in maieste with his fader? Credo.

Beleuyst þow þat he schal come at the day of dome to deme þe gode and þe badde? Credo.

Beleuyst þow in þe holi gost, the thridde persone in trinite, and in holy cherche, and þat þe sacrementis of holy chirche aren ordeyned in remissioun of mannys senne? Credo.

men þat bene saued; and fore gladnes of suche felauschip be þou of good confort in god, þynke how þow muste after þis lyfe leye a stone in þe waH of þe cite of heuene, sclely with outen noise or strife, and þerfore, or þou wende out of þis world, þou polisscH þi stoon and make it redi, ȝif þou wolt not þere be lettid.

¶ þis stoon is þy soule, whiche þou muste make stronge þorough right bileue; and faire þou muste hit clense, þorough hope of goddis merci and perfite charite, the whiche coueritH þe multitude of synnes. þe noyse . .——

ᵃ How a man schulde conforte annothere, þat he gruche nought when he is seke.

Broþer or sister, louyst þou god þi lorde? he or sche, ȝif þey may speke, woH sey 'ȝhee,' ᵇ or perauenture, ȝif þey may not speke, þenke 'ȝhee.'

¶ þan þus, ȝif þou lovest god . . . ᶜ ȝiffe detH goo faste on a man, Speke to hym thesse wordis.

Broþer or Systere in god, ȝif þou see or . . . . . .

ᵈ Now when þou hast seyde aH þis, or ȝif þow maist not seye aH for hastynge of detH, beginne here or his mynde go from hym.

Broþer or sister, art þou glad þat þow schalt dye in cristyn feythe?

---

¹ leaf 51.
ᵃ leaf 15, back. ᵇ leaf 16.
ᶜ leaf 18. ᵈ leaf 19, back.

From the Office for the Visitation of the Sick.

Beleuyst þow in þe sacrament of þe auter, þat is cristes bodi whiche was born of marie, wiche criste lefte her among vs as for þe most preciows iewel, whan he schulde departe be deth from his disciples?   R'. ʒhe. knowlechist þou . .   [*Rest missing.*]

Credo.

Beleuest þow þat alle tho þat been in good lif schul haue part of alle ¹the¹ gode dedys, and preyeres that been doon in holy chirche, and [þat] alle tho þat been knet to-gedere here in holy chirche be grace, schul ben knet to-gedere in euerlastyng ioye?

Credo.

Trustis thow in þe mercy of god, wiche wil not the deth of a synful man ʒif he be sory of hys senne and schreuen, and in wyl to amende hym?

Credo.

Trustis þow þat thow schal haue mercy ʒif þow be sori of þin senne?

Credo.

Trustis thow þat thow, and euery man and woman, schal rise vp at þe day of dome in body and in sowle, the badde to be dampned in endeles peyne, and þe gode to be take, bodi and sowle, in-to euerelastyng blisse?

²Credo.

Art þow in wil fulli to forʒeue alle maner of men and women that þat þey haue trespased to the, so that þow art in wil to kepe no rancowr ne malise to hym in þe herte, but to be in loue and charite with eche man and woman?

. . . ⸍ . . . .

I knowliche to god, and to owre lady seynt marie, and to alle þe halwen of heuene, that I haue senned, with mowth spoken, with feet goon, with eyen seyen, with eren hered, with nose smelled, with herte þowht, and with al myn senful body myswrowth; therfore i preye owre ladi seynt marie and alle the halwyn of heuene, prey for me; and the prest, þat thow beseche for me, and me asoyle, for charite.

ʒif the seke mai speke after that he is schriue, and hath mad his general confessioun, asoyle the prest hym on þis wyse.

---

¹⁻¹ In a later hand.   ² leaf 51, back.

From the Office for the Visitation of the Sick.

[1] Now, brodir or sister, ȝif þow beholde any cros, or ony ymage mad with mannes hond, wite wel þat it is not god; therfore thinke or seye in þin herte: I wot wel that þow art not myn god, but maked after hym, to make me haue more mynde on myn god; therfore, lord fader þat art in heuene, merci i aske of alle þe sennes that i haue trespased aȝens the wilful passioun of owre lord ihesu crist, the whiche he suffred for al mankende. merciful fader, of thi goodnesse and thi grete mercy, do awey al myn wikkednesse!

The General Sentence.

This form of excommunication, read four times a year, has been printed from an excellent text in the Early English Text Society's volume entitled *Instructions for Parish Priests*. The General Sentence is commonly found in the printed or later Manuals, but appears to have had no distinct place in any medieval service-book.

[1] leaf 52.

The manufacturer's authorised representative in the EU for product safety is Oxford University Press España S.A. of El Parque Empresarial San Fernando de Henares, Avenida de Castilla, 2 - 28830 Madrid (www.oup.es/en or product.safety@oup.com). OUP España S.A. also acts as importer into Spain of products made by the manufacturer.
Printed and bound by CPI Group (UK) Ltd, Croydon, CR0 4YY

23/03/2026

02075335-0001